Finding Joy

Finding Joy

Words to capture the beauty of ordinary life

Dearbhla Mescal

First published in the UK in 2026 by Eriu
An imprint of Bonnier Books UK
5th Floor, HYLO, 105 Bunhill Row,
London, EC1Y 8LZ

Copyright © Dearbhla Mescal, 2026
Illustrations © Steve Doogan, 2026

All rights reserved.

No part of this publication may be reproduced, stored or transmitted in any form or by any means, electronic, mechanical, photocopying or otherwise, without the prior written permission of the publisher.

The right of Dearbhla Mescal to be identified as Author of this work has been asserted by her in accordance with the Copyright, Designs and Patents Act, 1988.

This book is a work of Non-Fiction. Some names may have been changed to respect the privacy of those mentioned.

A CIP catalogue record for this book is available from the British Library.

Hardback ISBN: 978-1-80444-287-6
eBook ISBN: 978-1-80444-389-7

3 5 7 9 10 8 6 4

Design and Typeset by Envy Design
Printed and bound in Great Britain by CPI (UK) Ltd, Croydon CR0 4YY

Every reasonable effort has been made to trace copyright holders of material reproduced in this book, but if any have been inadvertently overlooked the publishers would be glad to hear from them.

The authorised representative in the EEA is Bonnier Books UK (Ireland) Limited.
Registered office address:
Block B, The Crescent Building
Northwood, Santry
Dublin 9, D09 C6X8
Ireland
compliance@bonnierbooks.ie
www.bonnierbooks.co.uk

Contents

Introduction — 1

Day
1. **Loving** — 5
2. **Living** — 11
3. **Hoping** — 15
4. **Being** — 19
5. **Wishing** — 23
6. **Trusting** — 27
7. **Choosing** — 33
8. **Sheltering** — 37
9. **Accepting** — 41
10. **Looking** — 45
11. **Knowing** — 49

12	**Finding**	55
13	**Owning**	59
14	**Seeking**	65
15	**Worrying**	69
16	**Beginning**	73
17	**Trying**	77
18	**Embracing**	81
19	**Sharing**	85
20	**Resting**	89
21	**Learning**	93
22	**Believing**	97
23	**Pausing**	101
24	**Shining**	105
25	**Mothering**	109
26	**Holding**	115
27	**Dreaming**	119
28	**Ending**	123

| Conclusion | 127 |
| Acknowledgements | 131 |

I would not be here – really here – without the care, skill and knowledge of my medical teams.
To my GPs: my original – Dr Christopher O'Rourke in Maynooth, now retired;
Dr Rosemary Keenan, who listened and heard; and Dr Maeve Byrnes in Celbridge, who continues my journey to health.
To Dr Patrick Hayden, my main man, and his teams in the Beacon and St James' Hospital.
Oh my goodness, how blessed I am to be in your care.

To Tracy McNamara, my oncology nurse, always there and still is.

To the entire army of souls filled with kindness who held me each Tremendous Tuesday in the Beacon and for my 'big stay' in the Burkitt Ward at St James', I have no words.
My heart will forever hold you and those you hold dear.
Thank you all.

&

To the pieces of my own heart who make me whole, who give flight to my dreams, make me braver and kinder and who always hold me safe.
Paul, Paul, Donnacha & Nell ...
You burst my heart wide open.

Introduction

Finding Joy came about after I challenged a friend to find joy in their life every day for twenty-eight days. I heard somewhere that if you reach twenty-eight days of anything it will become part of your daily practice.

So, picture this. Pitch side, the north wind is blowing, with spits of rain mixed in for good measure. It was around 2011; I was standing bundled up in my faithful football coat, hood tight-up at Hawkfield, when another mum sidled up beside me. We began to chat. She was going through some stuff and she was working full time with children still at home.

We turned towards each other, our faces cocooned in our hoods, blocking out the wind and the rain and focusing inwards to have this conversation. One that changed my life and I hope changed hers. She asked a question so many of us ask – *when is it going to be my time?*

I answered swiftly – 'Not now! Now, we *mother*. Now, we put our feet out, one in front of the other and keep pushing forward.' She looked at me and I knew I had to do better than this. So, I spoke from my heart what I wanted for her, for me and for all of us feeling the overwhelm of dreams not happening or roads getting bumpy. I told her we had to see the joy in the ordinary.

'You know when you come in tired and their shoes are all at the front door, or their washing hasn't actually made it into the machine and you want to kick the shoes and scream blue murder?' I said.

'Instead, see the shoes piled high as a blessing that all your babies are home before you and that you get to see them tonight. As you fold their laundry, know that when they put this jumper on, that a bit of your love is in the cuff.'

I suggested that for the next twenty-eight days, we would find three joys – simple easy joys. I listened more and spoke a bit more and she listened and for a few minutes we made plans to see our worlds a little different. We hugged and released our hoods to the howl of the wind. The last whistle blew and as I made my way to my car, I ruminated on this conversation and the challenge we had set each other.

So, twenty-eight days of finding joy began. I decided to document it on Facebook to hold myself accountable. I needed this challenge. Life was happening to me and I was playing catch-up all the time. I was seldom present.

I mean, I was there – but only there – with a map to the next place I was supposed to be.

Finding Joy was born and it became a commitment I made to myself. Over the years, I've become more honest and I have leaned into my vulnerability, of this much I am sure.

Joy became – or should I say – *curating* joy became part of my daily life. My children grew and I moved from Facebook to Instagram (I like it better there). My thoughts deepened and became more personal. The possibility of writing a book raised its head, but at this point each of my children were embarking on their lives outside of our walls. Nell leaving school and moving to London, Paul living out of a suitcase pursuing his career and Donnacha stepping into the corporate world with all its challenges.

Then the summer winds blew cancer my way and life kind of stopped.

Work came to a halt and every ounce of me took up the fight. My curated joys became so very important. They helped me see joy when my body could not get out to see them in real life. My *Finding Joy* practice had spread; people who have followed me sent me their simple joys – clothes blowing on a line in Shetland, daffodils by a river, sunrises, sunsets, jumping in puddles – there was so much joy falling into my messages and with them I felt lifted and permitted to see more than the four walls of the room I was in. I was filled with gratitude. I felt held and able to concentrate on getting better.

This little book is a cumulation of my curated joys throughout the past few years. It contains my rambling thoughts on life's issues that have popped up along the way. I truly, truly hope it gives you a pathway to beginning your own twenty-eight days of finding joy.

Day One

Loving

You were a whisper

Did you know
you were a whisper
I made to my heart?

Can you imagine
what happens when that whisper to the universe
comes true?

When a tiny hand
wraps around your finger
and takes hold of your heart?

Life
Life happens

You begin to live
in full colour

A rainbow connection
formed between
what was before
and the family we became

Imagine a life lived
when all our whisperings
all our lit candles
all our quiet moments
of dreaming and wishing
come true

It is time
to embrace the whole of our lives
and watch
as the colours deepen
with a life lived
with our hearts
and eyes wide open

The kiss

I waved from my row
you didn't see me

I blew you a kiss
at your bow
it never found you

I watched as you searched
your eyes locking hers
and my heart melted

The love you have
for each of our children
is all I ever wanted for them

To feel that kind of love
I believe
helps you love
helps you
navigate the world
and
all the loves
they will have in it

It's the love of stories
and fables
It's a love that shows up
that will hold you up
that will gather you
when the path is uneven
or if you are unsure

Yes
you missed my kiss
but I rejoice
in the joy of knowing
our children know
a love such as yours

Day Two

Living

A cocktail for life

Fill your soul with:

a cup of joy
a precious handful of friendships
a load of dreams
one straight-up love
a dollop of adventure
a dash of anticipation
a tumbler of butterflies
topped off by a sprinkling of sunlight
breaking though a rainbow sky

Wild abandonment

Live
with a sense of joy
and abandon

It's magically messy
and wonderfully scary
all at the same time

Embrace it all
feel it all

Be present
and be wild

Day Three

Hoping

Yoga mat

Imagining my mat
like a surfboard
on a sea of my worries

My head full of lists and plans
and always ever hopeful
that my mind will quieten enough
to hold my tree pose strong

Hope
I realise
is a little joy
I gift myself in each hour
of my days—
the days that dash away from me
with no pattern or calm

The tree
outside the front of our house
reminding me
things need to change

Hope
is dashes of tiny things
within the joys I seek
It's in the texts we share
making plans for next week
It's in the long goodbye
off a call
bye, bye, bye

Hope is in love
in the holding of hearts
in the cherishing of others
in the feeding of our birds
in our walks with our dogs
in the building of spaces in our homes for more
in the pulling up another chair at our table

Tomorrow
she fully opens
dazzling in the new day
allowing the raindrops
to be her crystals

Yes
to love nature
is to hope
to plant a garden
is to hope
and
to lie on a mat
is to hope

A hope

I hope
the whispers you make
to the universe
from your own heart
blow gently
across your soul
and let you soar
into your dreams

Day Four

Being

You are

You are love and light
dreams and magic

You are my inhale
and exhale—
the whole of my breath

You are the blink
of my eye
Focus and depth

You are far away
as close
as I have ever been

You are the sun
and moon
tide and beach

You are the whole of me
in parts
outside of me

I am blessed
because
you are

Come walk with me

Come walk with me
count from your heart

Walking
is where I allow my mind to travel
and my imagination to take flight

I pause often
to watch a bee hover
or a bird swoop
I get excited
at a dragonfly's dance
or the sight of wildflowers
in the actual wild

I hope you get to walk
where the toes of your runners
get damp from the dew
or the leg of your tracksuit
gets splatters of mud
from the puddles you jumped in

Don't race—
pause, breathe
take the photo
listen to the sounds about you
let them become
the playlist to your soul

Day Five

Wishing

I wish you time

Time
to sit
read
listen
and breathe

I hope you see
a film of dust
lit by sunshine
upon your record player—
the normalcy
of a life being lived
and celebrated

Don't rush
step gently
dance wildly
and live fully

Tail winds

Tail winds and gentle breezes
soft voices and booming tannoys
safe travels, soft landings

Eyes open, heart full

Adventures to be taken
memories to be made
treasures to be found

A life that is messy and full of magic
I wish you the world, every mountain, river and sea

I wish you sunsets to envelop you
sunrises to embolden you
and the cosiness of a roaring fire
to settle you in the arms of your love

Day Six

Trusting

The tack stitch

Tack stitch: a quick temporary stitching intended to be removed.
To easily hold, to seam, trim until it can be permanently sewn.

As a parent
I began with my firstborn
to tack the thread
which provides (and still does)
a guide
for me as Mum
and them as child

It is a touching stone for us—
To understand
we have known each other
before we held each other

There is no rule book
there is no map
just trust—
trusting who you are
trusting who you raised
trusting who they trust
will hold their hearts
like precious gems
Letting the tack stitch fall slack
allowing that feeling
that tug in your heart space

as a loop loosens
slipping away—
knowing with certainty
that the original stitch knot will hold
and its strength
is in its ability to stretch

The thread is but a guide for their hearts
and mine
to stay connected
under different skies

Letting things go to grow

Letting things go
means it gets messy—
it's hard
it's difficult
and sometimes sad

Oftentimes
letting go means accepting
that the road or path you are choosing
isn't one the others are taking—
that you may be alone
scared but determined

Or
that the road you are on
is not right for you and
you have to stop
and reassess

Be patient with yourself
At this point of your life
you must lean
into yourself

There will be joys
that will let you know
you are exactly
where you are supposed to be—
little nudges from the universe
that let you know
you are aligning with yourself

Unconcerned by others' opinions
and a permission
to unfold
to become

To take the road
that allows you
to be your true whole self

Day Seven

Choosing

Notes, stars, dreams and music

I have been gifted
a labyrinth of choice
to see and hear

My own children
fill their souls
with their gifts
and in my turn
I have learned
how to find my gifts
and permit my cup
to fill

There is a joy
in finding what you love
and letting it sit
within you

Time has allowed me
to delve within
to seek the notes
stars
dreams
and music
that set me alight

I have become aligned
and focused
with the gift of time

Make sure you make time
to hear the song of your soul

Be still and listen—
she is speaking

Hear her well

Glorious hope

Actively engage
in hopefulness

Our own hopes and dreams
leave a trace
of ourselves
on those we meet
love
and pass by

Let us be aware
of our choices

Let us walk
with gentle intent
speak
with impeccable honour
and act
in glorious grace

Day Eight

Sheltering

Be shelter

Be shelter, find shelter

There is always room, time
and energy to do more
for those who need it most

Be the port in the storm
We can set the table for more than
just ourselves

The holding place

I remember my mother's kitchen table
before I remember mothering

I remember it being a safe place
where my panic of not knowing was released
and
I could rub mistakes out with my sleeve

My mother's table was the sound of a kitchen working
A family's circle
holding secrets, allowing tears to fall and laughter to fly

Though replaced, the space it held never lost its soul
It allowed us to shelter in the mess of it all
It watched broken hearts fall and
be gathered

A space where big decisions have been made
and
still when I feel it might all be a little too much
I sit in the shelter of all it holds
and has held
for me and mine

Day Nine
Accepting

Accept

Be still
Don't flap
let stuff settle where it lands and
see what you need to do

if anything

Often, I am spinning in circles, trying to
ensure nothing falls so
I can say I didn't fail

Foolish me, I can't catch everything
I can't fix everything
I can own it and I can see what I can do better

So, I tell myself
Do your best
Don't panic
If it becomes overwhelming
breathe in, breathe out
and remember there is no failure in failing

Try harder, try different or
accept and try another way

Butterfly dances

I counter punch my thoughts
with little tricks
that blow the fog away

I put on music
I put pen to paper
and begin to write
words
sentences
phrases

I read some poetry
I go outside

I allow myself
to question why
to address the why
to accept the why

I allow myself
to become vulnerable
to the tangible emotion
of worry

A face-off

I try
not to blink first

Day Ten

Looking

Look closer

Look closer
See within

Take a breath
Take another

Close your eyes
Let the memory of colour
wash about

Feel the air
Hear the sounds

Hands at heart centre
Hold your head up high

We are here together
Taking each step

Let us hold hands
As we fall inward

True self, whole joy

As you look
in your mirror
let your gaze
your words
your thoughts
to yourself
be as gentle
as a feather
resting on the grass

Loving myself
getting comfortable
in my own skin
is perhaps
the most joyous
of my found joys

Day Eleven

Knowing

Knowing

Knowing where you are going to land
isn't always a given

Sometimes—
usually more often than not—
you just have to feel your way
trust your instincts
and give way
to the inner pull
that tells you
this is the way

Trusting ourselves
is the hardest job
our inner critic can be loud
but I am a work in progress
and my joy-beat
is getting loud
and sometimes—
yes, sometimes—
she beats that critic down

Finding my joys
in my everyday
helps me find
my landing spot

I hope you find
some joys each day
to
savour
share
and hold

That those joys
become the treasures
for those days
you may need them most

Being a girl

I am supposed
to know my cycle
I am supposed
to know my feelings

I am supposed to—
But what if I don't?

What if the moon
and the sun
the clouds
and the rain
the heat
and the cold
all collide?

Can I stop
pause
and connect
with myself?

Will I be able?
Will I like what I see?
Will I understand
my voice
my rage
my love?

Everything runs though me—
Glaciers
rivers
and seas

I am the sum
of the mountains
forests
and glades
I am earth, wind and fire

I am dark and light

I am it all

Day Twelve

Finding

Shifting into joy

Not every day is easy
I am not always at ease
I can feel on edge
like I am walking a tightrope
with no net

Finding joy
while walking a tightrope—
even on a good day—
is not easy
but on a day
where the rope is swaying
in the wind
everything becomes harder

So I go in search of joy
going where I have found joy before—
my garden
the birds
the wildness of it all

Moving into a joyous space
is a shift change
you begin to smile
and that joy
becomes contagious
within you

I try to remember
my happiness
is mine to own
and create

Joy

If you have it
hold it

If you see it
grasp it

If you need it
my wish for you
is that you find it

That you find it
in the ordinariness of a life well lived—
in a pile of folded laundry
in the wind blowing
through the trees
in a song
in the sound of laughter

and the feeling
of your heart exploding
in a long-awaited hug

Day Thirteen

Owning

Answer when you know

There are days
when the light seems perfect
It defines all it touches
allowing the smallest bud
to stand out

Maybe we should embrace
what makes us stand out—
that bit
which puts us first
and enables people
to see
the whole of us

I remember the child
that was me
waving wildly
in the classroom
excited beyond measure
because I knew the answer—
so excited
so proud of myself
only to be passed over

Oh, I still feel
the power of that pass over
but now
I don't need anyone's permission
to speak

I am here
I own my voice

I am still that little girl
who wants to be picked
but in this light
right now
I know what I say
is important to me
and though I may still be waving—
it's probably part
of a dance move

At the bed's edge

Speak to your children
of owning the day
they have just lived

If there is a worry held
help them see
how they could use their voice
to make their own hearts
feel less broken

Listening
to the words being spoken—
nothing is so big
if we share the load

Owning
is not shaming
owning
is standing tall
and letting the light in

At your most vulnerable,
worried and awake—
remember how
when you sat
on the bed's edge
of your little hearts
helping them see
a way through

That owning the dark
helps them to own
all the joy,
love
and light
that we create

To own
each corner
of the life
you are living

Owning
is accepting flaws,
relishing joys
and marvelling
at the wonder of you

Day Fourteen

Seeking

Let us seek

Let us seek joy in the ordinary
and
make our days extraordinary

Let us marvel
at the wonder
and
watch the sunflower grow

Let us see the rainbow
and
give thanks to the rain

Let us grasp the coffee cup
with both hands
and smile at the friends at our table

Joy begets joy
Very simply
when I open my eyes wide
I can see joy come falling in

My cup runneth over
my heart becomes full
and I am lifted
by the world I have created
around me

My fire
my chair
my books
my garden
my bird feeder
my cup
my thoughts—
my little world

Yes
let us seek joy
in the ordinary

Seeking is not selfish

Remember
that the universe is infinite
and our dreams
can come true
you just have to say
what you want
out loud

Seeking
isn't selfish
or silly
It is sitting quietly
with yourself
until suddenly
the picture presents itself

Seeking
is finding a way
to allow your passion
to thrive
your soul
to light up

To be the chooser
of your chosen life

Day Fifteen

Worrying

Honestly

Don't worry about
what you look like

Honest to goodness—
every one of us
is just
trying
to find our own toes

None-too-pretty thoughts

Out here in the open
with my negative thoughts—
my worries
the magnitude of it all

I can remove the self
I can begin to softly speak
tapping gently on my wrist to
allow myself
to become fully present

There is freedom
in acknowledging
and accepting
these none-too-pretty thoughts

I get to reassess
realign
and reemerge—
a little bit stronger
a little bit wiser

Day Sixteen
Beginning

Home

It is where we learn
Where we ran
walked
fell in love

It is the starting point
to everywhere—
and nowhere in particular

It sits in the centre of us
allowing us to catch our breath
weaving us back
pushing us forward

Home and the feeling of home are
the gifts we want to hold and give

A beginning of dreams
and a soft place to land

Let us carry a piece of home on our wings
as we travel far and remember often

Birthdays...

I am halfway there—
Wherever there is

I am a secret holder
a kindred spirit
My heart is full
but always with more space—
more capacity to love
and to be loved

I make a wish or two
and decide, here and now
to strive
to make them come true

We know love
we know how to love
Now
let the magic begin

Day Seventeen

Trying

The recoil of hurt

A friendship
I thought would be forever—
A delight to be in that place
of truth
love
and trust

But when it was taken from me
I was left dangling
trying to balance
my truth
with hers

I hid for a while
the hurt too raw—
curled up safe
within my own
story of it all

This is a life
lived in truth and light
my heart on my sleeve

The hurt
pain
and grief
at its loss in your life
is real

We can feel
the bittersweetness of it—
like a summer's end

Don't ever be so afraid
of the recoil
that you miss out
on the love
of a friend

Out of your depth

That feeling—
of being slightly out of your depth
but still in your power

The moment you try something new
feeling silly
but engaged

Oh! The magic—
you feel the grin grow
the positivity
of daring to do

We can
if we try
And trying
is truly
truly miraculous

Day Eighteen

Embracing

The butterfly effect

Butterflies inside
let me know life is exciting—
unexpected
and doable

I will always want
life to turn out perfect

They say with age comes wisdom
and that wise old owls
know life isn't perfect—
and that the imperfection of my life
often leads to unimagined joys
wonder
and magic

I cling like ivy
to a beautiful imperfect wall
knowing for certain
the butterflies inside will cease—
and
I will receive what I need
not always
what I thought I wanted

I stretch my arms
take a breath
and then
with grateful hands
accept the gifts
of the gentle flutterings within—
which bring me to the present moment
and allow me to embrace
the adventures yet to be had

Little seeds

I know where I can go
to quieten my mind

All these little seeds
of joyous knowledge
about myself

They enable me
to slip securely
into this time of my life

Where my adult children
come and go
spinning their own web of dreams
that glisten and shine

Where I can, without fear
embark on the parts of my life
that I want to explore
and embrace
with total uncertainty

I will jump
into this life of mine
with joy
and abandon

Day Nineteen

Sharing

Let the joy in

Let joy in
Find it
Curate it

Joy is an active emotion in my life
it does not make hard things go away
but it does help me navigate
through those tough times

Sifting through my joyous moments
gives me hope to hope
Even hoping for joy
is joyous

My wish is that
in sharing our joys
with those we meet
it might allow us
to see our lives
as extraordinary

Us

As the light switches on and off
on their stages—
flickering with anticipation
drive
and exhilaration—

I believe they know that
somewhere not too far away
is me:
ready when needed
but completely committed
to watching in delight
as a new circle is formed
around these hearts of mine

Based on love
and
a shared excitement
for a life
being fully lived

Day Twenty
Resting

May I give you rest?

What if the words I spoke were
May I give you rest?
How would it feel
to hear these words
on any given day?

Begin each day saying
May I give you rest?
to yourself

These words exude grace
calm
and love

If you said them to another
you would say it with such gentleness—
they would fall
like a sunbeam
through the trees

May I give you rest?
allows my thoughts to reset
my heart to beat slower
and my body to stop resisting

I become the words
I move with purpose—
in kindness

My thoughts become quieter
whispering to my soul
knowing that I am worthy
of the kindness
I bestow on others

May I give you rest?
May I give you rest?
May I give you rest?

Now is good

Be here now
be wherever here is for you
Be fully present
Carve out some time
Go gently in your day

Rest a while
on your comfy chair
in your favourite spot
Hear the silence
Feel its warmth

I have joy
I am joyous
I am hope-filled

I want the best for you—
because you at your best
makes me better

Together, we are stronger
Loving with peace and gentleness
brings us all
to a place of grace

Let us be filled with grace
Rest easy
on this day of days

Day Twenty-one

Learning

Learning

I am learning—
I am my own best friend

I affirm every day
joyous affirmations
setting my own soul on fire

I seek out good
actively
Be the extra
in every day

It has taken me
a long, long time
to get here

I was too busy
for too long
Felt I was too much
for too long

But what I am learning is
I am never too much
for myself

Being exactly who I am
keeps me joyous
keeps me authentic

Allows me to be fully present—
and kinder
more fulfilled

I am a better
all-round human
on this planet of ours
by being
my extraordinary self

Bowing

I have learned
how to say goodbye
say hello—

bow to the biggest hurts
and
embrace the incredible joys

Day Twenty-two
Believing

Pack wisely

I cannot stop
my anxious heart

Believing in something more—
having that north star as a guide
something to tether
our crazy spinning world to

What to do I believe in?
Hold true to?

Nature—
she adapts
she allows change to happen
she rewilds
she tells me
I will see more

I will feel something
Life can seem
so overwhelming

I remember
that a patch of grass
gets mowed often—
but still
the daisies come

I will be
a better packer
of the important stuff
I want to take
on this journey of mine

I believe in you

I believe in you—
the whole possibility of you
the magnificence of you

I hold your heart
your trust
the space of you
 as a sacred thing

To be the holder of your heart
is a gateway
to your dreams
hopes
and promise

I quieten my mind
and allow grace to settle

I hold the truths
between you and I—
each like a prism
open to light
able to cast
rainbows on the ceiling

Day Twenty-three

Pausing

It will pass

Pause—
and watch the birds
drink from the water fountain

Hear a song in your mind
that lends itself to help you
lean into the worry and stress
knowing:
it will pass

It always does

Look up, see more

I watch the clouds drift by—
and with a simple breath
and a gentle pause
joy comes sweeping in

Day Twenty-four
Shining

Shining

Me shining
shouldn't dim anyone else's light
Each of us
can become all that we wish for

What if all our actions
caused a positive reaction?
What if all our interactions
were based on kindness?

Yes, I know—
positively naïve
But I like to live—
live audaciously
to be ever hopeful

I engage in this world of ours with
the wisdom of my age
and the knowledge of my soul

I share my joys to cause a ripple effect
to lift up
to buff your spirit

Let's go bedazzle

Joy is a verb

Joy is a doing thing
I pile joy on
I get my happy on—
And joy comes flooding in

I wear my joy
and shine on

Day Twenty-five
Mothering

Mothering

At this stage in life
I am learning more
from my children
than they are from me

I have learned my blessing—
that when my children speak
from their hearts to mine
I sit deep in myself
and listen with intent

They are wise beings
these humans we rear

I am joy when I feel their love—
even if the words I hear
require a shift in me
a change of perspective
or a letting go
to become lighter in myself

Isn't that a lovely thought to have—
that by listening deeply
we can become lighter
freer perhaps
set a new course
see differently
see more clearly

Oh to be silent enough to hear love

Your room

The aroma of memories
the thrill of the rain
the tingle of sunshine
the shock of the wave—
all of these joys
bring me to your room

Yes it is still yours
although your 'stuff'
no longer lies on the floor

I see you
I feel you in this space
The smell of your body spray
lingers in my heart

I catch myself
as I walk past a particular shop
or a group of young people—
and I am struck
by the memory of you

I reach out
I reach back
I see you
as I pass your door
I tend to your room
as I do my garden—
placing a favourite flower
in amongst the wildness of things

You my wondrous child
my darling girl
piece of my heart
bring joy to all my senses

You are dappled light
and a clap of thunder
I sit on your bed
and feel you breathing

I am alive

Day Twenty-six
Holding

Staying connected

Some days are hard
I am listening
but I don't have the right words—
the right way
to say what I want to say

So I let the silence fall
The silence doesn't feel good
but it is a connection—
no matter how tenuous—
between you and I

I open my mouth to say something
then shut it tight
Maybe all I have to say
is nothing

That being here
at the other end
just holding this sacred space
is enough—
that it says it all

That saying nothing
validates your hurt
your upset
your anger
and troubles

That by saying nothing
I hope you know—
I am holding it all

Being grateful

Celebrate the body
that has you sitting
standing
running
jumping—

picking up
holding on
and letting go

Hold your belly—
yes hold it
smile in the mirror
and give yourself a wink

Clap your hands
wriggle your toes and
wobble those arms

Trust me—
there is so much to be grateful for
to love
and yes—
to hold

Day Twenty-seven
Dreaming

Unfolding

What happens
when you no longer need to be on the same page—
when two become one
to raise three?

What happens
when that one page
needs to become two again?

I did the one-page thing
with very little thought
it was easy for me—
I fold up well

So in becoming two
I folded up my page neatly
took hold of my side
of an imagined foolscap page
of dreams, hopes and wishes—
a map for a life
to be created of us

We each parented
boldly and defiantly
We dreamed
the biggest dreams possible

Now
my own folded page
is poking out—
and the parts of me
I had quietened
are beginning to make some noise

We are moving forward
unfolding

There is
so much to do
so much to see
and so much
more than we could ever have imagined

It is time

Dreaming

We still hold on
to our shared page—
and still get excited
by the dreaming of our hearts

But our own pages
get to uncrumple
take up space
sharing what was once
only held
in our own imaginations

My dreaming
has always nurtured me
kept my soul ticking

My time
our time
is now—
and the dreaming
is unfolding

Day Twenty-eight
Ending

Grab the good days

Grab the good days—
treasure them

Chances are
the good days are made up of small
seemingly trivial moments that
together make for an incredible day

So today
make time to take that photo
write your thoughts
sit with someone who needs you
send that text
make that call

I promise—
it will land right where you wanted it to

Time moves so fast
and we are all so very busy

Your kindness matters
And through our small acts of kindness
we can make a better day
a better week
a better month
and
a better life

Sweet summers end

Each part of my heart
is in one place—
for a brief moment
the sweetest of moments

The magic sound of laughter
that to my ear is pitch perfect
where every voice
is heart and matter

The washing machine spins
the house creaks
the piano plays—

and I will sleep softly

Conclusion

Hello!

If you've flicked straight to the back – welcome. I hope you've read even a little of the middle so you know this isn't a book of instructions or neat lists. It's a collection of thoughts, musings and ramblings – a daily gift I gave myself, a record of how finding joy transformed the way I live this life of mine. If you've skipped ahead that's okay too. You're here now and that matters.

When I first began recording my joys on social media, I remember walking with an old friend and saying, 'By five o'clock today I have to find a joy.' She replied, 'Well if you have to find it and it's not coming naturally, maybe it's not authentic?' Her words stopped me in my tracks. Was I being inauthentic? Was I performing for an audience? I hadn't even considered that possibility. At the time it felt innocent – just me trying to notice something good in the day. Yet from the very beginning people became invested in what I posted. They wanted to know what each joy, would be even though my photos were simple and unfiltered – wrinkles and all. I believed I was showing my real joys, not a curated version of life.

I understand her questioning though. Authenticity is fragile these days. We live in a world where everything is edited, filtered and fact-checked because we can't always trust what we see. We worry about safety, about oversharing, about whether what we put out there is real or some AI fabrication. That constant second-guessing robs us of something essential: the freedom to simply be.

What I realised then – and what I hold onto now – is that not all my joys will sit comfortably in someone else's space. This was self-work done in a public space and it won't be for everyone. But in my heart I knew the premise was real: to work on myself no matter how busy, how hard the day, how sad I felt. This magic potion of joy became solace – a way to keep going when life felt heavy. My thoughts became my joy; a daily point of happiness amidst chaos. They were never about perfection; they were about survival, about finding light when the dark pressed in.

Over time I've learned that I can live vulnerably and remain true to myself. I instinctively share my vulnerability so others feel safe in my company. Sometimes I overshare and sometimes I wonder, *Why did you say that?* But that's part of being open. My joys aren't a cure for anxiety – they won't heal the wounds – but they help me manage –

like a plaster. They won't make the pain disappear, but they soften the edges. I hope they do the same for you.

When cancer hit it felt like a wallop. It hit my family too – each of them living with the knowledge that while they were living, I was fighting. At the time I was too busy with the job at hand to think about their pain. Looking back, with space between then and now, I can feel their sadness and shock. I can imagine the weight they carried quietly while I carried mine.

We are talkers and sharers deeply engaged in each other's lives. Each Christmas we gather as five, raise our glasses and speak our hopes aloud. In sharing dreams we are at our most vulnerable. My children have seen us lean into tiny joys – the photos on the kitchen wall changed each January to reflect the year gone by. They smile at those memories and see what living in joy can do. They know that joy isn't loud or grand; it's often quiet, tucked into ordinary days.

We talk about tough stuff. We laugh easily, cry easier still. We fill each other's cups when we can't fill our own. My grandest joy is that our children like each other – truly like each other. That joy took root by letting disagreements happen, by listening, by not stepping in. So when curveballs like cancer landed they could lean on each other and let their heaviness be held.

Our circle grows as loves and friendships join in. I watch hearts explode with life – my cup runneth over. My children love fully and have friends who hold their hearts like crystal. That is joy times a million.

Living in joy, continuing to find joy every day is my practice. I photograph something on every walk. I print a million photos. I believe seeking joy – practicing twenty-eight days of joy at different times – alters my brain and makes me easier to be around. It's not about ignoring pain; it's about refusing to let pain have the final word.

Letting joy seep in is like letting a wild garden grow. It takes patience. It's messy and not what you hoped for – until suddenly there it is: a multitude of green with a dash of magic colour. Joy is like that – unexpected, unruly and beautiful.

Joys are the magic elixir of my life. As you close this page I hope you find three joys today – ones you might have missed – because you slowed down, focused and gifted yourself time. They don't have to be big. They don't have to be perfect. They just have to be yours.

Wishing you good things and a life of very ordinary extraordinary moments.

xx
Dearbhla

Acknowledgements

This is the scary, hard part that no one tells you about! Oh to not leave anyone out and also to not go on forever. I am one who reads acknowledgements because I always guessed it took an entire other world to help create a piece of work and I like to read who helped the writer bring their idea out into the great wide open!

So here is my little (or not-so-little) universe of kind hearts who listened, read, reread (I am sure a hundred times), guided and lifted me, held and hold me and love me unconditionally.

To Sheila Crowley of Curtis Brown for being beside me from the get-go, we are kindred spirits. Deirdre Nolan of Eriu, my editor and trusted partner. To Lisa Gilmour, assistant editor of Eriu, for all the help putting this together.

To Tamara Douthwaite, Sophie Raoufi and Clare Kelly of Bonnier Books for your tireless work, for your social media know-how and for trusting me in the process. To Helena Maybery of Curtis Brown for keeping me in the loop and updated. To Declan Heeney of Gill Hess for all the phone calls and happy news.

To Steve Doogan for your talent. Your art made a dream come true. To Nick Stearn who brought the cover design to life. To Miriam Mulcahy, author of *This is My Sea*, who took a call from me and made me feel that it was really possible – I did fill that white board!

This book was inspired by a conversation on the side of a pitch and I will always be grateful to that mum who caught me unawares and gave me pause. To all my side-pitch mums who bundled up tight in our matchday coats who gave me such joy and friendship – some which have lasted way beyond a three o'clock throw-in or kick-off.

To the friends I have garnered a little later in life, you are my touch stones of kindness and joy. To my mum, Marie and my dad, Colm ... you live within me. To my sister Eimear and my brother Colm Óg, we are bound and we are love. To my in-laws and out-laws, my grandaunts and uncles, my cousins, my nieces and nephews – you each inspire me and gift me a place called home.

To Paul, who has sat beside me on the darkest of nights, who has believed in this book way before I could believe in my ability to do it. You have my heart.

To my children, Paul, Donnacha and Nell, you taught me that living on the edge is fun and a little scary but your mentality of 'if you don't dare to dream, it can't happen' has allowed me to jump because I know that your arms are all outstretched to catch me. You are my safe place to land. You are the pieces of my heart outside my body and I love you beyond anything. I wrote a book, it took a universe. I was brave, I am vulnerable and I am forever grateful.